KU-165-515

Presented to

on the occasion of

With love from

Celebrating Retirement

Copyright © 1993 Mary Hathaway

The author asserts the moral right
to be identified as the author of this work

Published by
Lion Publishing plc
Sandy Lane West, Oxford, England
ISBN 0 7459 2396 8
Lion Publishing
1705 Hubbard Avenue, Batavia, Illinois 60510, USA
ISBN 0 7459 2396 8
Albatross Books Pty Ltd
PO Box 320, Sutherland, NSW 2232, Australia
ISBN 0 7324 0631 5

First edition 1993

All rights reserved

A catalogue record for this book is available
from the British Library

Printed and bound in Malaysia

Acknowledgments

Thank you to Roger Hall for the use of his piece 'Old
man in my youth', and to David Kossoff for his piece
from 'Young Mind', a 'sort of prayer', from *You Have A
Minute, Lord?*, published by Robson Books Ltd.

Photographs by Lion Publishing: pages 16, 21,
24 (top), 34/35; Nicholas Rous: page 27; Steve and
Mary Bevan Skjold: page 29; ZEFA UK: pages 17, 18,
20, 22, 23, 31; /Ken Schiff: endpapers; /Jeff Turnau:
page 7; /Paul Steel: page 13; /Bob Gelberg: pages 14/15;
/George Contorakes: page 36; /A. Edgeworth: page 37;
Kelly/Mooney: page 25; Telegraph Colour Library:
pages 30, 41; /J. Sylvester: pages 44/45; Tony Stone
Worldwide/Richard Elliot: pages 28/29; Neil Beer:
pages 12, 24 (bottom), 35, 42; Willi Rauch:
pages 19, 26, 43; Uniphoto: pages 32/33; Jon Arnold:
pages 38/39

CELEBRATING RETIREMENT

Mary Hathaway

A LION BOOK
Oxford · Batavia · Sydney

INTRODUCTION

Retirement comes at a time of transition in our lives. It brings changes and, inevitably, mixed feelings about what is being left behind and what is to come. I have selected pieces of my writing for this book with these feelings in mind, together with Bible verses and some of my favourite quotations.

Years ago, retirement meant the conclusion of a busy and often arduous working life, with the hope of rest and a quiet corner by the fire. These days nothing could be further from the truth! With increased medical care, people stay healthier and live longer and can expect a quality of life which would have amazed previous generations. So this time comes as a gift which should not be taken for granted. It is up to us what we do with it.

In society today, success seems to be measured by the activities that can be crammed in between waking and sleeping. The pace of life is frantic and ruled by the clock. It seems that unless you are living at eighty miles an hour you aren't really living at all! The amount any one individual can do appears to be more important than the kind of person they are.

Maybe retirement gives us a chance to redress the balance. There is time for relationships and a chance to stop and look at the world around us. It allows us to live life at depth instead of just rushing over the surface. It might, perhaps for the first time, help us to begin to understand what life is all about!

Change is never easy, and some find it harder to cope with than others. But change also brings hope and the opening up of new horizons. So with thought and planning, we can grasp the exciting opportunities that retirement brings, letting it enrich our own lives and those of people around us.

Mary Hathaway
January 1993

HERE'S TO THE NEXT STAGE!

For friends and colleagues to sign and send best wishes

23rd Psalm for busy people

The Lord is my Pace-setter, I shall not rush.
He makes me stop and rest for quiet intervals,
he provides me with images of stillness, which
restore my serenity,
he leads me in ways of efficiency, through calmness of mind,
and his guidance is peace.

Even though I have a great many things to
accomplish each day,
I will not fret, for his presence is here.
His timelessness, his all-important will will keep
me in balance.

He prepares refreshment and renewal in the midst
of activity
by anointing my mind with the oils of tranquillity.
My cup of joyous energy overflows.

Surely harmony and effectiveness shall be the
fruits of my hours,
for I shall walk in the pace of my Lord, and dwell
in his house for ever.

TOKI MIYASHINA, JAPAN

Don't be afraid or discouraged for I,
the Lord your God, am with you
wherever you go.

FROM THE BOOK OF JOSHUA

He sets ... the time for planting and the time for pulling up,
the time for tearing down, the time for building.

He sets the time for sorrow and the time for joy,
the time for mourning and the time for dancing.

He sets the time for finding and the time for losing,
the time for saving and the time for throwing away,
the time for tearing and the time for mending,
the time for silence and the time for talk.

FROM THE BOOK OF ECCLESIASTES

The gift of love

If I am on many committees
but do not love others,
I am simply making a useless noise.

If I have every enthusiasm for useful projects
but forget to love those for whom they are intended,
what good will it do?

If I do many good works to glorify myself
but do not love others,
I am worth nothing.

If I am altogether too busy organizing love
that I forget what love is like,
it will be of no value at all.

Committees will come to an end,
useful projects will become unnecessary.
Good works done from wrong motives will pass away—

but love is the one thing that will last for ever.

Trust in the Lord with all your heart. Never rely on what you think you know.
Remember the Lord in everything you do, and he will show you the right way.

FROM THE BOOK OF PROVERBS

We make our plans, but God has the last word.
You may think everything you do is right, but the Lord judges your motives.
Ask the Lord to bless your plans, and you will be successful in carrying them out.

FROM THE BOOK OF PROVERBS

Summer field

I was walking, with more time to spare than usual, through a summer field. The grass was quite long and blowing in the wind. As I looked around me I became aware of how many different kinds of grasses there were. Some had heads as sturdy as golden wheat, others were like plumes of feathers. Some were as delicate as finest lace and one kind of grass had seed heads so fine that they seemed to cover the ground with a purple mist. Ordinary grass is something that most people walk by without even noticing, but I realized that even grass has its beauty and each kind is sculptured individually in the hands of God.

Lift your eyes and look to the heavens:
Who created all these?
He who brings out the starry host one by one,
and calls them each by name.
Because of his great power and mighty strength,
not one of them is missing.

FROM THE BOOK OF ISAIAH

Slow me down, Lord! Ease the pounding of my heart by the quietening of my mind. Steady my hurried pace with the vision of the eternal reach of time. Give me, amid the confusion of my day, the calmness of the everlasting hills. Inspire me to send my roots deep into the soil of life's enduring values that I may grow towards the stars of my greater destiny.

Night fall

The night falls
softly like
a benediction
from the sky,
absorbing all
the colours
of the day.

All the brightness
and the bustle
of our busy doing
shrinks to silhouette
and shadow in the
gentle uniformity of grey.

The sky enlarges
in the stillness
to remind us of those
things beyond and all
our self-importance
fades away.

Warp and weft

Today I left my colleagues at work for the last time. I shall always be pleased to have news of them but I doubt if I shall stay in close contact with very many—and the rest? They are like the weft threads in a piece of cloth, woven in for a short time but not there for long. So many people come and go in my life. Sometimes they weave in very beautiful colours, but they don't stay forever.

So while I thank God for everything these people have given me, I am most thankful for those who have stayed with me over the years, who know me best and love me most, for these relationships are constant and very precious. Like the warp threads in a cloth, they seem to hold my life together. But beyond them I am thankful for God's love which undergirds me like the loom itself. For without him there would be no shape or meaning to my life and there would not be any cloth woven at all.

Jesus Christ is the same yesterday,
today and for ever.

FROM THE BOOK OF HEBREWS

Every good gift and every perfect
present comes from heaven; it comes
down from God, the Creator of the
heavenly lights, who does not change
or cause darkness by turning.

FROM THE BOOK OF JAMES

Crafted by hand

In our sitting room is a wooden plaque which we treasure. It shows Mary, holding the infant Jesus, with Joseph beside her. It was made by a man whose hobby has been woodcarving for many years.

I saw a similar one in his home and liked it so much that I asked for a copy. When it arrived, the figures were not in traditional clothes as in the original. Mary was wearing a dress and shawl and Joseph a duffle coat and flat cap! I realized that our friend is unable to make an exact copy of anything. He really enjoys what he does, and each piece he carves is unique.

In this age of mass production and synthetics, it is a privilege to own something that is crafted by hand, and made out of natural materials.

I am the true vine, and my Father is the vinegrower. He removes every branch in me that bears no fruit. Every branch that bears fruit he prunes to make it bear more fruit . . .

Just as the branch cannot bear fruit by itself unless it abides in the vine, neither can you unless you abide in me. Those who abide in me and I in them bear much fruit, because apart from me you can do nothing.

FROM THE GOSPEL OF JOHN

Constant care

We moved to a house with a large garden.
Fired with enthusiasm I found a magazine
which advertised a wonderful selection of
seeds as a special offer. I put in my order, my
mind filled with dreams of perfect flowerbeds
full of beautiful blooms. The seeds duly
arrived and in the spring I planted them. To
my delight they actually came up, from every
single packet, and I watched over them
anxiously. Then I planted them out and
watered them faithfully every night until they
were well established. Just before we went on
holiday in the summer they were beginning to
flower and I was really pleased with myself!

But we were away for nearly two weeks
when the weather was at its hottest. When we
got back the garden looked like a desert. The
lawn was brown and most of my carefully
nurtured plants had simply dried up and were
completely dead. I was bitterly disappointed
after all the work I had put into growing
them.

Well, I learned the hard way. To get the
most out of a garden, of course, it needs care
and attention all the time—not just when it's
convenient or we happen to feel like it!

Shelter

Draw the curtains,
shut out the night.
Make a shelter
for light and warmth
against the cold.

Give love time
to grow here.
For every lamp
needs protection
against the storm,
somewhere it can
burn quietly and steadily,
gathering strength
before it goes out
into the rain,
the wind and the dark.

Let love grow unseen
in the shelter of this home.
And then there will be light enough
not for this home only,
but to stream out
into the world.

I have cared for you from the time you were born.
I am your God and I will take care of you until you are old
and your hair is grey. I made you and I will care for you;
I will give you help and rescue you.

FROM THE BOOK OF ISAIAH

Children need the wisdom of their elders;
the aging need the encouragement of a
child's exuberance.

ANON

The old man in my youth

My grandfather had two corner-lined distant eyes and leathered skin. These came from scanning distant horizons and turning foursquare into the biting wind. He was ever looking beyond the farthest point of view, expecting there would be a sail or something else.

My grandfather had strong hands, hardened by salt and sea water, hands good at tightening spars and turning spanners. He found it difficult to pick up beads . . . and babies. But they were kind fingers with a firm grip, even when they took you by the ear.

Grandfather had a weatherbeaten mind, he faced nature's fury better than the new fangled. And he rejoiced in yesterday. Today and tomorrow would, he supposed, take care of themselves. His armchair was there yesterday and was one of life's few certainties.

For all his distant look and hardened hands and impatience with tomorrow, kindness looked out through his eyes and there was grace in his touch.

ROGER HALL

C OMPANIONSHIP

Giving

Thank you for spending time with me,
listening to my thoughts
and giving me encouragement and understanding.

Thank you for putting yourself out
and changing your plans
so that you could fit me in.

Thank you that you know
that to share your possessions
is only the beginning.

For what you have given me
is far more costly—

it is the gift of yourself.

People learn from one
another, just as iron
sharpens iron.

FROM THE BOOK OF
PROVERBS

Growing old

The signs of age
that others see
mean little as
you look at me.

For much I've seen
upon your face
has slowly turned
to inward grace.

If all that counts
is stored within,
what matter if
the shell grows thin?

For then the light
shines clearer through—
so all I see
is simply you.

And behold, the Lord passed by, and a great and strong wind rent the mountains, and broke in pieces the rocks before the Lord, but the Lord was not in the wind; and after the wind an earthquake, but the Lord was not in the earthquake; and after the earthquake a fire, but the Lord was not in the fire; and after the fire a still small voice.

FROM THE FIRST
BOOK OF KINGS

Look up at the stars

Look up at the stars
in the winter cold,
for they are bright
and pure and touched
with the remoteness
of eternity.

Look up at the stars
in the summer night,
for they are warm
and tender, bending
down with passionate
caress.

Look up at the stars
in the autumn dusk,
for they are rich
and mellow, growing
in the sky as fruits
of love.

Look up at the stars
in the dawn of spring,
for they are young
and free and laugh
for joy to see
the world reborn.

Be still, and know that I am God!

FROM THE BOOK OF PSALMS

Loneliness

Loneliness comes in sudden storms
that have to blow themselves out.
Loneliness does not always bow to reason.
Loneliness is a continuing pain,
it can strike without warning.
Some loneliness can be shared
but it is only a sharing of the loneliness,
not the dispersing of it.
Loneliness can look out of anguished eyes
into love, and not know how to let love in.
Love does not hold the key to loneliness.

But love remains—
and will wait until the darkness passes.

Be content with what you have; for he has
said, 'I will never leave you or forsake you.'
So we can say with confidence, 'The Lord is
my helper; I will not be afraid. What can
anyone do to me?'

FROM THE LETTER TO THE HEBREWS

My life is changing

My life is changing. The old, safe routines are gone and there are more spaces than there used to be. I have made plans to fill them but I'm not sure how it's all going to fit together. I know that change can be a good thing but it can also be a little frightening. I don't like being at a loose end while I sort everything out—it makes me feel lonely and a bit insecure. But if I try to fill all the gaps at once, I know I shall make mistakes.

So I will try and be patient, believing that God knows and cares about me and what I do with my life. Then with his help, each part of the plan will fall into place and become something beautiful and of value to many.

L IFE IS FOR LIVING

Joy in old age

You have taught me ever since I was young,
    and I still tell of your wonderful acts...
Now that I am old and my hair is grey,
    do not abandon me, God!
Be with me while I proclaim your power
and might
    to all generations to come...

I will indeed praise you with the harp;
 I will praise your faithfulness, my God.
On my harp I will play hymns to you,
    the Holy One of Israel.
I will shout for joy as I play for you;
    with my whole being I will sing,
    because you have saved me.

FROM THE BOOK OF PSALMS

Yesterday is a memory, tomorrow has
not come. Give joy today to as many as
you can.

ANON

With God all things are possible.

FROM THE GOSPEL OF MATTHEW

It can't be done

According to the theory of aerodynamics, as may be demonstrated by wind tunnel experiments, the bumble bee is unable to fly. This is because its size, weight and shape in relation to the total wing-spread make flying impossible.

But the bumble bee, being ignorant of these scientific truths, goes ahead and flies anyway: and makes a little honey every day.

ANON

The big dark

When my son was two he discovered what he called
'the big dark'. He had been up much later than usual,
so it was dark before he went to bed. He was
fascinated and quite awed by this immense darkness
that we called 'night'. He wanted to see just how far it
stretched so I had to go with him into every room of
the house and out of the front door and the back, so
he could see for himself just how far it went. It was as
he feared—it filled his known world! However hard I
tried to convince him that it would be gone in the
morning he would not believe me and went to bed in
a very worried state of mind.

Early next morning he trotted into our bedroom
as fast as he could to tell me that the light had come
back. But he was still suspicious and I had to get up
and go with him into every room and out of the front
door and the back before he was satisfied that the 'big
dark' had really gone. We had to continue this
routine, night and morning, for several days until
finally my small son accepted the inevitable turning of
night and day.

I remember smiling because he could not
understand something which was so obvious to me.
But then I thought of my own times of darkness and
how I had cried to God in despair, thinking that they
would last for ever. Yet they always did pass
eventually. Perhaps God smiles very lovingly at me
when I can't understand things that are so clear to
him—because both dark and light do fit into his
pattern in the end.

Your word is a lamp to guide me and a
light to my path.

FROM THE BOOK OF PSALMS

The Lord is the everlasting God;
　　he created all the world.
He never grows tired or weary.
　　No one understands his thoughts.
He strengthens those who are weak and tired.
Even those who are young grow weak;
　　young men can fall exhausted.
But those who trust in the Lord for help
　　will find their strength renewed.
They will rise on wings like eagles;
　　they will run and not get weary;
　　they will walk and not grow weak.

FROM THE BOOK OF ISAIAH

33

The inn

We were having a lovely day out in the country when we happened to drive past an old pub. We decided to call back there for our evening meal.

When we arrived later we found that the building was indeed old, dating back to the thirteenth century. The fireplace was the original one and there was a deep incision in one of its stones which travellers had used to sharpen their knives.

We sat by the welcoming blaze of the open fire, as we waited for our food to be served. I placed my hands on the ancient stones and felt them throb with the living of all who had flowed past them throughout the centuries. On cold nights, road-stained travellers must have gathered round this same fireplace. What stories did they tell as they mellowed in its warmth, trying to outdo one another until the candles were snuffed out? So many lives intertwined, just touching for one brief evening and then going their separate ways, probably never to meet again.

And still the fire lived on. It seemed as if the air was filled with voices from long ago, mingling with the dance of the flames. But like them we could only briefly stay—yet we were glad to be a part of this stream of history.

We, who are rich and privileged,
thank you for the gift of leisure,
for time to unwind, reflect and plan,
to exercise or simply sit in quiet.
We thank you for the people who create our
holiday
by working in the cockpit and control room,
in garage, signal-box and harbour office;
for those in kitchens, dining-rooms and bars,
those guiding tours and running sports and games;
may they too find time for rest and recreation...
May we be truly recreated in our recreation,
our lives enlarged with new enthusiasm
and a broader vision of your purpose.

STEPHEN ORCHARD

The gift of people

Be careful
with butterflies
for they are fragile
and easily damaged.
Do not think
you could manage
readily without them.
It is not for you to say.
For they are bound up
with you in the pattern of life
and their brief and beautiful
existence is precious
in the eyes of God.

Be careful
with people
for they are fragile
and easily damaged.
Do not think
that some are more
important than others.
It is not for you to say.
For we are here to serve
and not to rule
and the bruised and easily
broken ones are precious
in the eyes of God.

Old friends

As I get older, it's not easy to keep in touch with all my friends and family. People move around so much and those that go back to the beginning of my life are getting fewer in number.

Old friends understand because they were there. I don't have to explain things to them or fill in the gaps. Other people may think they understand but when I see the look on their faces I know I am asking too much of them.

Old friends are precious, and time given to bulding up relationships brings a rich reward.

Friendship is a flower

Friendship is a flower
that grows in many places,
sometimes in a hollow
protected from the storm.
But it can be found
out upon the hillside,
rooted all the deeper
for the blowing of the wind.

Friendship is a flower
rare and very precious
for flowers close their petals
till opened by the sun.
And thoughts remain as buds,
only blossoming in sharing,
until the warmth of love
gently touches every one.

The pilgrimage

Light has always
been embroidered
on to darkness.

Rainbows have always
been seen
against the clouds.

Beauty has always
dwelt alongside
ugliness.

Winter and spring
have always gone forward
hand in hand.

Pain, fear and chaos
have always been the backcloth
for love, joy and peace.

Do not be afraid,
for this is the way of things
and how it has been
since the beginning.

The world is no worse,
much may have changed
but the root of the problem
is always the same.

Beauty and laughter
can be found in your world
as much as they always have,
it just depends where you look.

Do not be afraid to follow them—
your pilgrimage will not be wasted.

Prayer at eventide

I bring Thee now, O God, the parcel of a
completed day. For I have wrapped it in
my thoughts, tied it with my acts, and
stored it in the purposes for which I live.

As the evening falls and while I seek
Thy face in prayer, grant unto me the joy
of good friends, the curative power of
new interests, the peace of a quiet heart.
Bestow upon me, Eternal Spirit, light as
darkness comes—
Light not of the sun but of the soul, not
for the eye but for the mind.
Light by which to judge the errors and
the wisdom of the day's work.
Light for the path that the soul must
find in the tangled ways of coming days.
And grant Thou again the healing touch
of sleep. Amen.

PERCY ROY HAYWARD

Ladders

Why are we obsessed with climbing ladders?
Ambition is not a bad thing. It's only when it gets
too important that it becomes a problem. But it's
easy to slip into the standards of those around us.
Careers are considered to be so important, 'You
can't have fulfilment unless you get on in your
career,' we are told. Is climbing the career ladder, on
its own, really the route to happiness?

Careers only last until retirement and then there
aren't any ladders left to climb. Some people find
that difficult, especially if all their lives they have
been told they must get to the top, because even if
they have got there, where do they go then?

Perhaps we should be trying to climb a different
ladder altogether, one which is based on eternal
values rather than society's. For to God every person
is equally important. It doesn't matter what kind of
work we have done or how successful we have been.
God loves us for what we are.

Learning to love like this is of more value than
anything else we do in our lives, and it may be that it
is the only ladder that leads to real happiness.

Do not store up riches for yourselves here on earth, where moths and rust destroy, and robbers break in and steal. Instead, store up riches for yourselves in heaven, where moths and rust cannot destroy, and robbers cannot break in and steal. For your heart will always be where your riches are.

FROM THE GOSPEL
OF MATTHEW

The gift of wonder

However much
I think I know
about the universe,
however clever
I think I may be,

if I cannot look up
at the stars
and simply wonder,
then I miss the purpose
of their very existence.

For they are,
first of all,
fingerprints of God.

So, Lord, please keep me young in the mind.
    Let me enjoy, Lord, let me enjoy.
If creaky I must be, and many-spectacled,
    and morning-stiff and food-careful,
If trembly-handed and slow-moving and
    breath-short and head-noddy,
I won't complain. Not a word.
If, with your help, dear Friend, there
    will dwell in this ancient monument
A Young Mind. Please, Lord?

DAVID KOSSOFF

The flower cluster

Each tiny flower
perfection,
each alone
in its loveliness
yet linked
in a cluster
of beauty.

Creamy white petals,
crisp with youth,
that flush pink
as they grow older—
it seems they
gather beauty
at the sunset
of their lives.

So Lord, grant to me
that I may become
more beautiful
as I grow older,
and may the sunset
of my life
be lit up
by the beauty
of eternity.

Look back and give thanks.
Look forward and take courage.

ANON

YOUNG AT HEART

But the path of the righteous is like the light of dawn,
which shines brighter and brighter until final day.

FROM THE BOOK OF PROVERBS

Facing the future

I want so much to live every stage
of my life positively and creatively.
Lord, you have always guided me
with your love and wisdom. I
cannot believe that this will change
just because I am getting older.

I ask you now to help me face
the future with courage, faith and
joy. Help me not to run away from
its problems but to face up to
them with you so that we can
triumph over them together.

Yet all experience is an arch wherethro'
Gleams that untravell'd world, whose margin fades
For ever and for ever when I move.
How dull it is to pause, to make an end,
To rust unburnish'd, not to shine in use!

TENNYSON, *ULYSSES*

I thought that my voyage had come to its end—at
the last limit of my power—that the path before me
was closed, that provisions were exhausted and the
time come to take shelter in silent obscurity! But I
find that Thy will knows no end in me. And when
old words die out on the tongue, new melodies
break forth from the heart. And when old tracks are
lost, a new country is revealed with its wonders.

RABINDRANATH TAGORE